Navigating the Maze of Creativity

MOHAMED FAWZI ELGENDI

WWW.FAWZOOZ.AI

NAVIGATING THE MAZE OF CREATIVITY

Copyright © 2024 Mohamed Fawzi Elgendi

No part of this work may be reproduced, distributed, transmitted in any form or by any means, including photocopying, recording, or other electronic or mechanical methods, without the prior written permission of the author, except in the case of brief quotations embodied in critical reviews and certain other noncommercial uses permitted by copyright law with the source duly credited. The names, characters, businesses, places, events, locales, and incidents are either the products of the author's imagination or used in a fictitious manner. Any resemblance to actual persons, living or dead, or actual events is purely coincidental.
www.mohamedfawzi.net

NAVIGATING THE MAZE OF CREATIVITY

Table of Contents

Preface 5

Understanding Your Innate Creativity 8

The Art of Applying Ideation Techniques 14

Crafting Your Creative Space 21

Navigating Through Challenges 28

Integrating Creativity into Daily Life 35

Emerging Trends and Technologies 41

Building and Nurturing Creative Networks 48

Case Studies of Innovation in Action 54

Conclusion 62

Creative Exercises 64

ABOUT THE AUTHOR 71

PREFACE 2024
WWW.MOHAMEDFAWZI.NET

NAVIGATING THE MAZE OF CREATIVITY

Preface

Welcome to "Navigating the Maze of Creativity," an expedition into the essence of innovation and the boundless capabilities of the creative mind. This publication serves as a guide, illuminating the paths through the complex world of creative thought and practice.

In these pages, we unravel the mysteries of creativity, from debunking common myths to exploring effective strategies for generating ideas and overcoming challenges. Each chapter is a beacon, designed to spark the innovator within and encourage a journey of personal and professional growth.

Beyond individual exploration, this series highlights the power of community in the creative process, showcasing how collaboration and diverse perspectives enrich innovation. Real-world examples across various fields demonstrate creativity's transformative impact, proving its universal relevance.

NAVIGATING THE MAZE OF CREATIVITY

As you engage with this series, embrace the opportunity to reflect, experiment, and create. "Navigating the Maze of Creativity" is more than a collection of insights; it's an invitation to become an active participant in the ever-evolving narrative of creativity.

Embark on this journey with an open mind and let it guide you to new horizons of imagination and ingenuity. The journey begins now.

CHAPTER 1
UNDERSTANDING YOUR INNATE CREATIVITY

Understanding Your Innate Creativity

In the labyrinth of life, creativity acts as a compass, guiding us through uncharted territories of challenges, opportunities, and personal growth. Yet, many of us question the presence of this compass within us, bogged down by myths and misconceptions. This chapter embarks on a journey to demystify creativity, helping you to recognize and harness your innate creative potential.

Unveiling Creativity

Creativity isn't just about painting masterpieces or composing symphonies; it's the spark that fuels problem-solving, innovation, and the ability to view the world from multiple perspectives. It's in the way you improvise a meal with limited ingredients, devise a new approach to a routine task, or find common ground in a complex negotiation.

The Myths of Creativity

Myth 1: "Creativity is an inborn talent" — While genetics play a role, creativity is largely a skill that can be nurtured and developed. Like a muscle, it grows stronger with use.

Myth 2: "Creativity is only for the arts" — Creativity transcends disciplines. It's equally vital in science, business, education, and daily life problem-solving.

Myth 3: "I'm not creative" — Everyone has creative potential. The difference lies in how we express and cultivate it.

Self-Assessment: Discovering Your Creative Strengths

To tap into your creativity, start with self-reflection. Consider moments when you've felt most creative, regardless of the outcome. What were you doing? How did it feel? This exercise isn't about validating your creativity with external achievements but recognizing the internal process and joy it brings.

Exercise: Mapping Your Creative Moments

1. **Reflect**: Think of three instances where you felt creative. These could be professional projects, personal hobbies, or even everyday tasks.
2. **Describe**: Write a brief description of each moment, focusing on your thoughts, emotions, and actions.
3. **Analyze**: Look for patterns in these moments. What environments, activities, or mindsets seem to foster your creativity?
4. **Plan**: Based on your analysis, brainstorm ways to integrate similar conditions or mindsets into your daily routine to nurture your creativity.

Cultivating Creativity: Beyond Innate Talent

Understanding your creative strengths is just the beginning. Cultivation is key. Here are some foundational practices to start with:

- **Diverse Experiences**: Expose yourself to new experiences, ideas, and perspectives. Creativity thrives on diverse inputs.
- Routine Breaks: Regularly step out of your routine. Even small changes can spark creativity.
- **Creative Play**: Dedicate time for unstructured, playful exploration in areas of interest. This can be as simple as doodling, experimenting with recipes, or tinkering with gadgets.
- **Mindfulness and Reflection**: Practices like meditation, journaling, or walks in nature can clear mental clutter, allowing creative insights to surface.
- **Embrace Failure**: View failures as learning opportunities and stepping stones to creative growth.

In conclusion, navigating the maze of creativity begins with recognizing the compass you hold within. By debunking myths, understanding your creative strengths, and adopting practices to nurture your creativity, you can enhance your ability to innovate, solve problems, and enrich your personal and professional life. Remember, creativity is not a destination but a journey — one that is uniquely yours. Embrace it, and let your creative compass guide you to realms of endless possibilities.

WWW.MOHAMEDFAWZI.NET

Navigating the Maze of Creativity

2024

CHAPTER 2

THE ART OF APPLYING IDEATION TECHNIQUES

The Art of Applying Ideation Techniques

In the vast expanse of the corporate and creative world, the quest for the next groundbreaking idea is relentless. The ability to weave the golden thread of innovation through the fabric of ordinary thinking separates the leaders from the followers. This journey of transformation is underpinned by a myriad of ideation techniques, each a beacon guiding through the fog of conventional thought. This chapter delves into the art of applying these ideation techniques, offering insights on how to harness their power to navigate the complex maze of creativity effectively.

The Human-Centric Approach: Design Thinking

At the heart of innovation lies empathy, the cornerstone of Design Thinking. This approach reimagines problem-solving through the lens of human experience, making it indispensable in sectors where the end-user's satisfaction is paramount.

Companies in technology, healthcare, and consumer goods can particularly benefit from this technique, crafting products and services that not only meet functional requirements but also touch the chords of human emotion and need.

The Creative Torrent: Brainstorming

The timeless technique of Brainstorming remains a potent force in unleashing collective creativity. Its beauty lies in its simplicity and inclusivity, inviting a deluge of ideas without the dam of judgment. For industries where volume and variety of thought fuel innovation — such as advertising, marketing, and creative design — brainstorming sessions can become the crucible for the alchemy of ideas.

The Alchemist's Code: SCAMPER

Innovation often involves the transmutation of the old into the new, a process meticulously captured by the SCAMPER technique. This methodical approach to tweaking existing concepts finds its stronghold in industries like manufacturing and software development, where iteration and enhancement are the keys to staying ahead.

The Cartographer's Vision: Mind Mapping

For those who navigate the world through visuals, Mind Mapping offers a compass. Its non-linear, visual approach to organizing thoughts and ideas makes it a powerful tool for creative fields such as content creation, advertising, and product development, helping to chart the course from conception to realization.

The Ensemble of Thought: Six Thinking Hats

Diversity in perspective breeds innovation, a principle embodied by the Six Thinking Hats technique. By donning different 'hats' — each representing a distinct mode of thinking — teams in management, strategy, and organizational development can explore the multifaceted nature of challenges, leading to more holistic and robust solutions.

The Archeology of Problem-Solving: The 5 Whys

Digging deep to unearth the root cause of issues is the essence of The 5 Whys technique. Its application is particularly transformative in process-oriented sectors like manufacturing and logistics, where identifying and addressing foundational problems can lead to significant improvements in efficiency and quality.

The Inventor's Blueprint: TRIZ

TRIZ serves as a blueprint for systematic innovation, drawing on the patterns of problem-solving in technological history. Its structured approach to overcoming inventive challenges makes it a powerful ally in R&D, engineering, and technology sectors, where groundbreaking solutions can redefine market landscapes.

The Realm of Possibilities: Provocation

Provocation techniques invite the mind to wander into realms of unconventional thought, making them a potent catalyst for creativity in fields driven by originality and differentiation, such as product design and advertising. By challenging the status quo, these techniques pave the way for groundbreaking ideas and solutions.

The Strategic Panorama: SWOT Analysis

Navigating the strategic landscape requires a clear understanding of one's position, strengths, and vulnerabilities. SWOT Analysis provides this panoramic view, making it an essential tool for business strategy, competitive analysis, and marketing, helping organizations identify innovative paths for growth and improvement.

The Narrative Journey: Storyboarding

Storyboarding translates ideas into visual narratives, making complex concepts accessible and engaging. Its application extends beyond filmmaking to user experience design and service delivery, where illustrating the customer journey or service flow can illuminate opportunities for innovation and enhancement.

In conclusion, the art of applying ideation techniques is akin to mastering a diverse palette of paints, each with its unique hue and texture. The skillful blending and application of these techniques can turn the canvas of ordinary thought into a masterpiece of innovation. As organizations and individuals navigate the complex maze of creativity, embracing these techniques with an open mind and adaptive approach will unlock doors to new possibilities, driving progress and success in the ever-evolving landscape of business and creativity.

WWW.MOHAMEDFAWZI.NET

Navigating the Maze of Creativity

2024

CHAPTER 3

CRAFTING YOUR CREATIVE SPACE

Crafting Your Creative Space

Having explored the essence of creativity and the myriad techniques to harness it, we now turn our focus to the environment — both physical and metaphysical — that fosters innovation. This chapter delves into crafting your personal Innovator's Workshop, a sanctum where creativity is not just welcomed but thrived.

The Physical Space: Designing for Creativity

The spaces we inhabit significantly influence our creative energies. Whether a corner of a room, a dedicated studio, or a digital workspace, the key lies in intentional design.

Elements of a Creative Space

- **Light and Nature**: Incorporate natural light and elements of nature. Plants, for instance, can boost mood and creativity.

- **Organized Chaos**: While some thrive in minimalist spaces, others find inspiration in a controlled chaos — think mood boards, idea maps, and open projects. Find your balance.
- **Tools at Hand**: Keep the tools of your trade within easy reach. The less friction between you and your creative work, the better.
- **Personal Touch**: Your space should reflect your identity and inspire you. This could mean artwork, inspirational quotes, or artifacts from your travels.

Exercise: Space Audit

Take a moment to assess your current creative space with the above elements in mind. What changes can you make to transform it into a more inspiring environment?

The Mental Space: Cultivating a Creative Mindset

The landscapes of our minds are as crucial as our physical environments. A cluttered, stressed, or rigid mind can stifle creativity.

Strategies for a Creative Mindset

- **Routine Detox**: Shake up your daily routine to prevent mental stagnation. Even small changes can spark new ideas.
- **Mindfulness Practices**: Meditation, yoga, or simple breathing exercises can help clear mental clutter, making room for creativity.
- **Curiosity Feeds Creativity**: Adopt a learner's mindset. Be curious, ask questions, and explore areas outside your expertise.

- **The Power of Pause**: Regular breaks, especially those involving nature or physical activity, can rejuvenate your mind and spark creativity.

Exercise: Mindfulness Break

Schedule a 10-minute mindfulness break into your day. Use this time to meditate, doodle aimlessly, or simply sit quietly. Notice any shift in your mental state post-break.

The Collaborative Space: Embracing Community

Creativity often flourishes in the presence of diverse perspectives. Building a community — virtual or physical — where ideas are exchanged freely can significantly enhance your creative output.

Building Your Creative Community

- **Networking and Events**: Attend workshops, seminars, and social gatherings within your interest areas.
- **Online Communities**: Join forums, social media groups, or platforms dedicated to your field of interest.
- **Collaborative Projects**: Engage in projects that require teamwork. The synergy of a group can lead to unexpected creative breakthroughs.

Exercise: Community Engagement

Identify one community or group within your field of interest and actively engage for a week. Share your ideas, ask for feedback, and contribute to discussions.

In conclusion, crafting your Innovator's Workshop involves more than just physical space — it's about cultivating a conducive environment in your mind and within your community. By intentionally designing your surroundings,

NAVIGATING THE MAZE OF CREATIVITY

nurturing a flexible and open mindset, and engaging with a community of like-minded individuals, you create a fertile ground for creativity to blossom. Remember, the environment you create is not just a backdrop for your work; it's an active participant in your creative journey.

WWW.MOHAMEDFAWZI.NET

Navigating the Maze of Creativity

2024

CHAPTER 4
NAVIGATING THROUGH CHALLENGES

Navigating Through Challenges

In our journey through "Navigating the Maze of Creativity," we've now arrived at a crucial waypoint: overcoming creative blocks. Every innovator, artist, and thinker encounters these hurdles, where inspiration seems like a distant mirage, and ideas refuse to materialize. This chapter explores the nature of creative blocks and offers strategic pathways to navigate through these challenging phases, ensuring that your creative voyage continues unimpeded.

Understanding Creative Blocks

Creative blocks are not just a lack of ideas; they're often the result of underlying factors that stifle creativity. These can range from emotional and psychological barriers to environmental and physiological triggers.

Common Sources of Creative Blocks

- **Emotional Barriers**: Fear of failure, perfectionism, and the pressure to perform can paralyze creativity.
- **Mental Fatigue**: Overwork and lack of rest can lead to burnout, leaving little energy for creative thought.
- **Environmental Stagnation**: An uninspiring environment or routine can dull the creative spark.
- **Information Overload**: Constant bombardment with information can overwhelm the mind, making it difficult to focus and generate original ideas.

Strategies for Overcoming Blocks

The key to overcoming creative blocks lies in identifying their source and applying targeted strategies to dismantle them.

Tackling Emotional Barriers

- **Embrace Imperfection**: Remind yourself that the creative process is inherently messy and that every attempt brings you closer to a breakthrough.
- **Mindfulness and Self-Compassion**: Engage in practices that reduce stress and foster a kinder, more forgiving attitude towards yourself.

Recharging Mental Batteries

- **Structured Breaks**: Integrate short, regular breaks into your work routine, using techniques like the Pomodoro Technique.
- **Detox Days**: Schedule regular days off from all forms of work and digital devices to allow your mind to rest and recover fully.

Refreshing Your Environment

- **Change of Scenery**: Alter your workspace or move to a new location temporarily to gain a fresh perspective.
- **Nature Immersion**: Spend time in nature, as natural environments have been shown to boost creativity and reduce stress.

Managing Information Overload

- **Information Fast:** Periodically limit your consumption of news, social media, and even reading to clear your mental landscape.
- **Focused Deep Work:** Allocate specific times for deep, uninterrupted work, using techniques like time-blocking to enhance focus and creativity.

Practical Exercises to Overcome Creative Blocks

Exercise 1: The Idea Jar

- **Preparation:** Write down random words, themes, or concepts on slips of paper and place them in a jar.
- **Practice:** Whenever you're stuck, draw a slip and use the word or theme as a prompt to sketch, write, or brainstorm, no matter how unrelated it may seem.

Exercise 2: The Creative Sabbatical

- **Plan**: Set aside a day or even a few hours where you engage in activities entirely unrelated to your usual creative work. This could be hiking, visiting an art gallery, cooking, or learning a new skill.
- **Purpose**: The aim is to give your mind a break from its routine patterns and stimulate it with new experiences and sensory inputs.

NAVIGATING THE MAZE OF CREATIVITY

In navigating through the maze of creativity, encountering blocks is a rite of passage. Rather than viewing them as insurmountable obstacles, consider them opportunities to pause, recalibrate, and gain deeper insights into your creative process. By understanding the nature of these blocks and equipping yourself with strategies to overcome them, you ensure that your creative journey is not just about reaching the destination but also about embracing the richness of the journey itself.

WWW.MOHAMEDFAWZI.NET

Navigating the Maze of Creativity

2024

CHAPTER 5

INTEGRATE CREATIVITY INTO DAILY LIFE

Integrating Creativity into Daily Life

As we continue our series "Navigating the Maze of Creativity," we arrive at a pivotal realization: creativity isn't confined to isolated moments of inspiration or the boundaries of traditional art forms. Instead, it's a way of living, a lens through which we can view and interact with the world around us. This chapter explores practical ways to weave creativity into the fabric of our daily lives, turning mundane tasks into opportunities for innovation and self-expression.

Embracing Daily Creativity

Creative living is about finding novelty and expressing oneself in everyday activities. It's the art of turning the ordinary into extraordinary by infusing it with your unique perspective and imagination.

Daily Habits for a Creative Life

- **Morning Pages**: Begin each day with a stream-of-consciousness writing exercise to clear your mind and capture fresh ideas.
- **Creative Commutes**: Use your daily commutes as a time for observation and ideation. Instead of scrolling through your phone, observe your surroundings and let your mind wander creatively.
- **Cooking with Creativity**: Transform cooking from a chore into a creative experiment. Challenge yourself to create new dishes with whatever ingredients you have on hand.

Cultivating Creativity in the Workspace

Your professional environment, whether at home or in an office, is fertile ground for creative practices. Integrating creative thinking into your work can lead to innovative solutions and enhanced job satisfaction.

Strategies for Workplace Creativity

- **Idea Lunches**: Organize regular lunch meetings where team members can discuss new ideas or share interesting findings, free from the pressure of immediate implementation.
- **Creative Challenges**: Set up weekly or monthly challenges that encourage thinking outside the box, such as finding new uses for common office items or brainstorming unconventional marketing strategies.

The Role of Rest and Play

Creativity flourishes not just in active pursuits but also in moments of rest and play. Balancing productivity with leisure is crucial for maintaining a creative flow.

Balancing Productivity with Creativity

- **Scheduled Downtime:** Deliberately schedule time for activities that have no purpose other than enjoyment and relaxation. This could be anything from painting to playing a musical instrument or gardening.
- **Playful Exploration:** Dedicate time to explore new hobbies or revisit old ones without any goal other than to enjoy the process and see where it leads.

Long-Term Creative Practices

Beyond daily habits and work strategies, there are long-term practices that can sustain and nurture your creativity over a lifetime.

Sustaining Creativity

- **Continuous Learning:** Commit to lifelong learning, whether through formal education, workshops, online courses, or self-directed study. New knowledge and skills can spark creative ideas in unexpected ways.
- **Journaling:** Maintain a regular journaling practice, not just for recording events but for reflecting on experiences, emotions, and ideas. This can be a rich source of creative material.

In Conclusion Integrating creativity into daily life is about shifting perspectives and embracing the possibility of innovation in every aspect of our existence. By adopting creative habits, inviting play into our routines, and committing to lifelong learning, we can live more fulfilling lives and contribute to a more innovative world.

WWW.MOHAMEDFAWZI.NET

Navigating the Maze of Creativity

2024

CHAPTER 6
EMERGING TRENDS AND TECHNOLOGIES

Emerging Trends and Technologies

In the penultimate chapter of our "Navigating the Maze of Creativity" series, we turn our gaze forward, to the horizon where emerging trends and technologies redefine the boundaries of creativity. As we stand at this juncture, it's crucial to understand how these advancements will shape our creative expressions, processes, and the very essence of innovation in the years to come.

The Digital Renaissance: Technology as a Creative Catalyst

The digital age has ushered in a renaissance of creativity, where technology acts not just as a tool but as a partner in the creative process. From AI-driven design to virtual reality (VR) experiences, technology expands our creative possibilities, enabling us to explore new realms of expression and interaction.

Artificial Intelligence: The New Muse

AI is transforming creative industries, offering tools that can generate art, music, and literature, or enhance human creativity by providing inspiration and assisting in the creative process. Platforms like DALL-E and GPT demonstrate the potential for AI to collaborate with humans, creating works that are a fusion of human ingenuity and machine intelligence.

Virtual and Augmented Realities: Expanding Creative Spaces

VR and augmented reality (AR) technologies are opening up new dimensions for creativity. Artists and designers are no longer confined to traditional canvases and mediums; they can create immersive, interactive worlds that offer novel experiences to their audiences. From virtual art galleries to AR-enhanced performances, these technologies are redefining the way we create and consume art.

Sustainability and Creativity: Crafting a Greener Future

As global awareness of environmental issues grows, sustainability has become a key driver of innovation. Creatives are at the forefront of this movement, using their skills to raise awareness, propose solutions, and imagine a more sustainable future.

Eco-Innovations: Art with a Message

Artists and designers are increasingly using their work to comment on environmental issues, employing sustainable materials and practices to create pieces that not only inspire but also educate. This trend extends to all creative fields, challenging professionals to consider the environmental impact of their work and explore greener alternatives.

The Collaborative Revolution: Creativity in the Age of Connectivity

The internet and social media have revolutionized the way creatives collaborate and share their work. Crowdsourcing, co-creation, and open-source projects harness the collective power of the global creative community, leading to unprecedented levels of innovation and diversity in creative outputs.

Crowdsourcing Creativity: The Wisdom of the Many

Platforms that allow for crowdsourcing ideas and solutions are democratizing creativity, enabling anyone, anywhere, to contribute their insights and skills to a common goal. This collective approach to creativity leverages diverse perspectives, leading to more inclusive and innovative outcomes.

Preparing for the Future of Creativity

To thrive in this evolving landscape, creatives must be adaptable, continuously learning, and open to experimenting with new technologies and methodologies. The future of creativity will be characterized by its fluidity, the blurring of boundaries between disciplines, and the fusion of technology and human imagination.

Embracing Continuous Learning

The rapid pace of technological advancement means that continuous learning is essential for anyone looking to remain relevant in creative fields. Engaging with new technologies, attending workshops, and participating in online forums are just a few ways to stay informed and inspired.

Experimentation and Adaptability

The willingness to experiment and adapt to new tools and platforms will be key to leveraging the full potential of future creative trends. Creatives must be open to exploring uncharted territories, using emerging technologies not just for their novelty but for their ability to enhance and expand the creative process.

In Conclusion As we peer into the future of creativity, it's clear that the interplay between technology, collaboration, and sustainability will shape the next wave of innovation. By embracing these trends and preparing for the changes they bring, creatives can ensure that they not only keep pace with the times but also contribute to a more innovative, inclusive, and sustainable world.

WWW.MOHAMEDFAWZI.NET
Navigating the Maze of Creativity
2024

CHAPTER 7
BUILDING & NURTURING CREATIVE NETWORKS

Building and Nurturing Creative Networks

In this chapter of our "Navigating the Maze of Creativity" series, we delve into the heart of creativity — not as a solitary endeavor, but as a communal journey. The creative community, with its rich tapestry of perspectives, skills, and experiences, is a crucible for innovation and inspiration. This chapter explores the significance of creative networks, offering guidance on building and nurturing these vital connections.

The Importance of Community in Creativity

The notion of the lone genius, toiling away in isolation, is a persistent myth. In reality, creativity thrives in the presence of others, drawing from the collective well of ideas, feedback, and support. A vibrant creative community can:

- Inspire: Exposure to diverse works and thought processes sparks new ideas and approaches.

- Motivate: Seeing others create and succeed provides encouragement and sets a benchmark for excellence.
- Support: The creative journey is fraught with challenges; a community offers emotional support and practical advice.

The Collective Brain: Synergy in Creativity

When creatives come together, they form a 'collective brain,' where ideas can be shared, expanded, and refined. This collaborative environment fosters a synergy that can elevate individual work to new heights.

Building Your Network: Connecting with Fellow Creatives

Creating a network doesn't happen overnight, but with intention and effort, you can cultivate a rich community of like-minded individuals.

Online Platforms and Social Media

- Joining Online Forums and Groups: Platforms like LinkedIn, Reddit, and specialized forums host communities for virtually every creative field.
- Social Media Engagement: Use platforms like Instagram, Twitter, and Pinterest to share your work, follow other creatives, and participate in discussions.

Offline Connections

- Workshops and Conferences: Attend events related to your field to meet peers and learn new skills.
- Local Meetups and Art Collectives: Join or form local groups that meet regularly for critique sessions, collaborative projects, or simply to share ideas.

Collaborating on Projects

- Open Calls and Collaborative Projects: Participate in or initiate projects that require collaborative effort, offering a chance to work with others and learn from their expertise.

Nurturing Relationships: Beyond Networking

Building a network is the first step; maintaining and deepening these connections is where the true value lies.

Regular Communication

- Stay in Touch: Regular check-ins, even if brief, keep relationships alive and show your genuine interest in others' work and well-being.
- Share Opportunities: If you come across opportunities that might benefit someone in your network, share them. Generosity strengthens relationships.

Collaborative Mindset

- Be Open to Collaboration: Approach relationships with the mindset of what you can offer, not just what you can gain. Collaborative projects can be especially enriching.

Feedback and Support

- Constructive Feedback: Offer and seek feedback in a constructive, respectful manner. A trusted critique partner can be invaluable.
- Support in Times of Need: Be there for your community members during setbacks or creative blocks, just as you would appreciate their support.

WWW.MOHAMEDFAWZI.NET

Navigating the Maze of Creativity

2024

CHAPTER 2

CASE STUDIES OF INNOVATION IN ACTION

Case Studies of Innovation in Action

In the culmination of our series "Navigating the Maze of Creativity," we turn our attention to the real-world embodiments of innovation. Through the lens of diverse case studies, this chapter illustrates the transformative power of creativity across various fields, offering insights and lessons that you can weave into your own creative endeavors.

Case Study 1: The Revival of a Brand — LEGO

Background: Once on the brink of bankruptcy, LEGO transformed through a strategic embrace of creativity and innovation, both in product development and customer engagement.

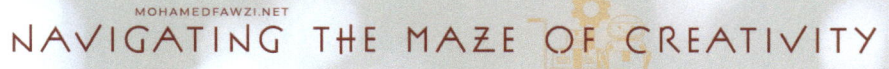

Creative Strategies

- **User-Driven Innovation:** LEGO harnessed ideas from its dedicated fan base, leading to the LEGO Ideas platform where users submit and vote on new set concepts.
- **Diversification:** Beyond traditional sets, LEGO expanded into video games, movies, and educational programs, broadening its appeal and market.

Lessons Learned

- Engage your community in the creative process; their insights can lead to groundbreaking ideas.
- Don't be afraid to diversify and explore new mediums of expression or business models.

Case Study 2: A Revolution in Music — Spotify

Background

Spotify changed how we access and enjoy music, moving from ownership to streaming, and in the process, reshaped the music industry.

Creative Strategies

- **Data-Driven Personalization**: Utilizing vast amounts of user data, Spotify created personalized listening experiences, making music discovery effortless and engaging.
- **Partnerships and Collaboration:** By collaborating with artists and record labels, Spotify ensured a win-win, fostering a sustainable ecosystem.

Lessons Learned

- Leverage data creatively to enhance user experience and engagement.
- Collaborative partnerships can be a key to innovative solutions and industry-wide shifts.

Case Study 3: Transforming Transportation — Tesla

Background

Tesla's ambition went beyond creating electric cars; it sought to revolutionize transportation through innovation in sustainability and technology.

Creative Strategies

- **Innovation in Product and Process**: Tesla's direct-to-consumer model and focus on sustainable energy have set new standards in the automotive industry.
- **Autopilot and AI:** Investing in AI and autonomous driving technologies, Tesla is paving the way for the future of transportation.

Lessons Learned

- Innovation can be a holistic process that includes product, service, and business model.
- Long-term investment in cutting-edge technologies can position a company as a leader in its field.

Case Study 4: A New Wave in Filmmaking — Pixar

Background

Pixar Animation Studios redefined the animation industry with its groundbreaking storytelling and technological advancements.

Creative Strategies

- **Story is King**: At Pixar, story and character development take precedence, with technology serving the narrative.
- **Fostering a Creative Culture**: Pixar's open, collaborative culture encourages risk-taking and values every team member's contribution to the creative process.

Lessons Learned

- Prioritize storytelling and emotional connection in creative projects; technology should enhance, not overshadow, the narrative.
- Cultivate a creative culture where ideas are freely shared, and failure is seen as a step towards innovation.

In Conclusion: The case studies of LEGO, Spotify, Tesla, and Pixar illustrate the multifaceted nature of creativity. Whether reinvigorating a beloved brand, revolutionizing an industry, or telling stories that touch hearts, the underlying principles of innovation, engagement, collaboration, and storytelling shine through.

2024

CONCLUSION
WWW.MOHAMEDFAWZI.NET

NAVIGATING THE MAZE OF CREATIVITY

Conclusion

As we conclude our journey through the maze of creativity, remember that these principles are not confined to businesses or creative professionals. They are universal, applicable in our personal lives, communities, and any endeavor we undertake. Let these stories inspire you to unleash your creativity, to see possibilities where others see obstacles, and to embark on your own path of innovation. In the realm of creativity, we are all explorers, and the map is yet to be drawn.

2024

EXERCISES
WWW.MOHAMEDFAWZI.NET

NAVIGATING THE MAZE OF CREATIVITY

Creative Exercises

Idea Generation Marathon

To push the boundaries of your creative thinking and generate a large volume of ideas for a chosen problem or project:

Select a Focus: Choose a problem or project you're passionate about.

Set the Stage: Create a comfortable, distraction-free environment. Have your favorite idea-recording tools ready (notebook, digital app, voice recorder).

Timer Setup: Set a timer for 60 minutes.

Idea Generation: Start the timer and begin jotting down every idea that comes to mind, no matter how outlandish. Aim for quantity over quality.

NAVIGATING THE MAZE OF CREATIVITY

Review: After the time is up, review your ideas. You'll find that the depth and originality of ideas increase as you move beyond the obvious solutions.

The Reverse Thinking Exercise

To use counterintuitive thinking as a catalyst for creativity, by exploring the worst solutions before arriving at the best ones:

Define the Problem: Clearly state the problem you're tackling.

Worst Ideas First: Spend 15-20 minutes writing down the worst possible solutions you can imagine.

Analysis: Review these 'worst ideas' and discuss (with yourself or others) why they are terrible.

Flip the Script: For each bad idea, consider what its opposite might be, or how you could tweak it into a viable solution.

Creative Constraints Challenge

To foster innovation by working within specific limitations:

Choose Your Constraints: Pick a creative task (e.g., design a product, write a story) and apply constraints (e.g., limited materials, word count).

Brainstorm: Within these boundaries, brainstorm as many ideas or solutions as possible.

Create: Develop your ideas into a finished product, adhering strictly to the constraints.

Reflect: Consider how the constraints influenced your creative process and the final outcome.

Mind Mapping Workshop

To visually organize thoughts and explore the connections between different concepts related to a central theme:

Central Theme: Write down the central theme or challenge in the middle of a large paper or digital canvas.

Association: Draw branches from the central theme to represent related sub-themes or ideas.

Expansion: Further branch out from each sub-theme with more specific ideas or solutions.

Visualization: Use colors, icons, or images to enhance the mind map and stimulate additional connections.

Action Plan: Identify actionable ideas from your mind map to explore further.

The SCAMPER Method

To creatively improve or innovate on an existing product, service, or process using the SCAMPER technique:

Select an Object: Choose an existing product, service, or process to improve.

SCAMPER Through: Apply each SCAMPER element (Substitute, Combine, etc.) to your chosen object, brainstorming as many ideas as possible for each category.

Evaluation: Review the ideas generated and identify those with the most potential for further exploration or development.

Prototype: If possible, create a simple prototype or plan based on the best ideas.

2024

AUTHOR
WWW.MOHAMEDFAWZI.NET

NAVIGATING THE MAZE OF CREATIVITY

me@mohamedfawzi.net
Dubai, UAE

Mohamed Fawzi Elgendi

AI Enthusiast & Mental wellness Author

Pioneering Digital Innovation, AI Advancement, and Cybersecurity Excellence.

Chief Information Security Officer (CISO)

Chief Digital and AI Officer (CDAO)

Post Graduate Program in Artificial Intelligence For Leaders

Bachelor's degree in Computer and Systems Engineering

400+ Enterprise project

70+ Training & Workshop

17+ Authored books

16+ Years Experience

- CBT COACH
- EQ
- DBT
- SCRUM
- ISO27001
- DATA SCIENCE
- BUSINESS OF AI
- DIGITAL PRODUCT DEVELOPMENT
- EXECUTIVE LEADERSHIP
- ENTREPRENEURSHIP

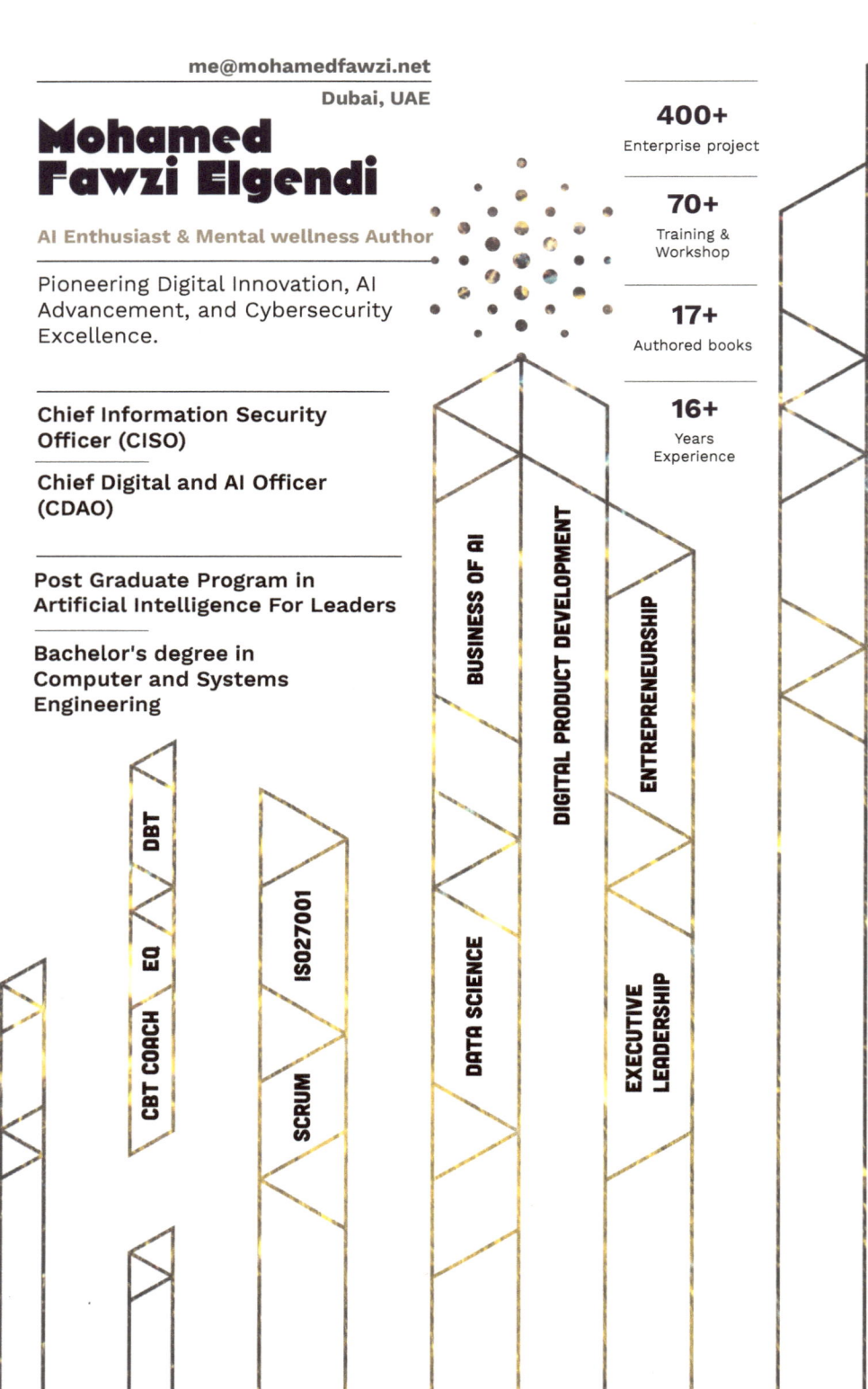

www.ingramcontent.com/pod-product-compliance
Lightning Source LLC
Chambersburg PA
CBHW040229220526
45473CB00001B/173